Beauty for Ashes

Biblical Help for the Sexually Abused

by John Coblentz

Christian Light Publications, Inc.,
Harrisonburg, Virginia 22802
© 1999 by Christian Light Publications, Inc.
All rights reserved. Published 1999
Printed in the United States of America

09 08 07 06 05 04 03 02 01 00   6 5 4 3 2

Cover Design: David Miller

ISBN 0-87813-584-7

CONTENTS

INTRODUCTION

The effects of sexual abuse are being felt not only in the world, but unfortunately in the church as well. And there is also a rising amount of help being offered to the abused. This help usually comes from support groups, from counseling, or in printed form. Often the abused benefit from all three. But unfortunately, the quality of help varies widely. Not all support is equal. Not all counseling gives the same answers. Not all books on the subject agree.

What is offered on these pages is intended to be a Biblical guide to the subject. The approach is not technical, but practical. The material is laid out in two sections. First, there is a concise description of the problems associated with sexual abuse, based on the story of Tamar. The second section is a guide to positive steps toward healing.

This book does not replace the need for human beings in the lives of the abused. Hurting people need more than bandages. They need more than sound advice. They need real people filled with the love and wisdom of God. They need people who will sit with them and listen, understand, and grieve with them. They need people who are not afraid to walk with cripples, people who are not embarrassed to see deformities, people who have the courage to face human sin and feel human pain. This is a guide. It is not a replacement.

This guide is addressed to Christians. It proceeds with the assumption that its readers have a living relationship with Jesus Christ and believe the Bible. It does not attempt to deal with legal aspects of sexual abuse, although sexual abuse is a crime, and law enforcement is provided for protection and punishment. This guide, instead, focuses on the inner needs of the sexually abused and those relational needs that fall within the responsibility of God's people and that are described in God's Word. In other words this is a Biblical guide, not a legal guide.

—John Coblentz

PART I
Understanding Sexual Abuse

What is abuse?

Abuse occurs when one person inflicts physical, emotional, or psychological damage on another person, especially in a relationship where love is expected. There are forms of abuse other than sexual abuse:

1. *Verbal abuse:* may occur through name-calling, belittling, harsh criticism, sarcasm, mockery, condemnation, or threatening. The damage is done by words and felt in the heart.

2. *Physical abuse:* may occur through excessive spanking, debilitating punishment, or hitting, pinching, etc., causing wounds or bruises. The damage is done by hands, feet, or other instruments and is felt in the body and in the heart.

3. *Emotional abuse:* may occur through inflicted guilt, rejection, playing on fears, abandonment,

1

or playing the martyr. The damage is done by one person tweaking the emotions of guilt or fear in another person. This keeps the first person in control, and the controlled person in continued emotional distress.

4. *Sexual abuse:* may occur through rape, incest, fondling, spectator sex, exposing oneself to others, introducing others to pornography or sexually explicit materials, verbally invading another's sexuality (either in jest or manipulation).

Sometimes sexual abuse is accompanied by one or more of the other forms of abuse as well. This is especially likely when the abuser is an older person and the abused is a child. Verbal or emotional pressure or both are commonly used to enforce silence about the abuse.

What happened to Tamar?

To understand sexual abuse, we will look at an example in the Bible. What Amnon did to Tamar is recorded in 2 Samuel 13:1-20. The following points summarize the tragic story:

1. Amnon was a half brother to Tamar. Both

were King David's children, but they had different mothers. Tamar's full brother was Absalom.

2. Amnon became infatuated with Tamar, but he knew he could not likely have her because he was her half brother. So he moped.

3. A friend of Amnon sympathized and suggested a scheme for getting what he wanted from Tamar.

4. Amnon pretended to be sick. When his father, David, visited him, Amnon asked David to tell Tamar to care for him in his sickness.

5. Tamar came to care for Amnon and took pains to serve him well.

6. When she brought food to Amnon, he asked all the servants to leave. Then he pulled Tamar into bed with him.

7. Tamar protested, but Amnon forced her and had sexual relations.

8. Afterwards, Amnon ordered Tamar out of the house. The Bible says his hatred for her then was stronger than the love he had had for her before.

9. Tamar was distressed beyond words. She had been forced. She had been violated. She had been shamed. She had been rejected. In her distress she put ashes on her head, tore her

3

clothes, and went home weeping.

10. Absalom, Tamar's brother, found out what had happened. He was furious at Amnon (and later killed him in revenge), but he tried to comfort Tamar. His method, however, was typical of many well-meaning comforters. He downplayed the terrible situation. "Hath Amnon thy brother been with thee? but hold now thy peace, my sister: he is thy brother; regard not this thing" (2 Samuel 13:20).

What makes sexual abuse so devastating?

Tamar was emotionally devastated by what Amnon did to her. If we look closely at what happened, we can see a number of reasons why sexual abuse is so painful:

1. *Tamar's abuse was painful because it came from someone who should have protected and loved her.* Amnon was Tamar's half brother. A brother should protect his sister. If anyone else would have made improper advances toward Tamar, Amnon would probably have protected her fiercely. He would have defended her against

other dangers. But instead of caring for her, he sinned against her.

Most sexual abuse comes from an abused person's relatives. The closeness of the relationship is used as a means to intimacy. And that is exactly what worsens the pain. When a stranger hurts us, we have the hurt to deal with. When we are hurt by someone whom we know and trust, we have not only the hurt, but a wounded relationship besides. Any memories of good associations darken under the cloud of being used. The very closeness of the relationship deepens the pain of the abuse.

2. *Tamar's abuse was painful because it confused love and selfishness.* Amnon said he loved Tamar. Amnon probably thought he loved Tamar. Amnon actually may have once loved Tamar. But as his desire for her grew, his love for her diminished. He came to want her for himself. Somewhere his love turned to selfishness and hid behind a mask of love.

Besides, what Amnon did to Tamar was designed by God to be one of the deepest expressions of love between a man and a woman. In a marriage where love has been cultivated and nurtured, the sexual relationship is a wonderful expression of love. But when a person uses a relationship to get sex, it is selfishness, not love.

Tamar felt the pain of being the object of Amnon's selfish desire. She felt it through an act that should be associated with the most tender attention and understanding from a man. By confusing selfishness and love, Amnon made Tamar feel like a disposable scrap of humanity instead of a cherished woman.

Typically, an abused person has trouble distinguishing between love and selfishness in future relationships. Once a person has been used for the selfish pleasure of an abuser, he or she finds it hard to trust the love of a true lover. Loving advances will be suspected of covering selfishness.

3. *Tamar's abuse was painful because Amnon played on her sense of obligation.* Amnon pretended to be sick. Tamar gave her time and energy to prepare a meal for him. She gave him something of herself. While she offered kindness and sacrifice, Amnon used her loyalty, her friendship, and trust toward him to get what he wanted. At the very time she was giving him what was good and right, he was scheming to rob her of what was not rightfully his. Part of Tamar's horror was realizing that her kind service had been part of his evil design.

4. *Tamar's abuse was painful because it associated powerful negative feelings with closeness.* Closeness in a brother-sister relationship should be associ-

ated with such warm feelings as understanding, kindness, security, acceptance, trust, protection, loyalty, and joy. Closeness in sexual union between husband and wife should have all of the above, only in greater degree. With Amnon's abusive action, however, Tamar felt exactly the opposite. In closeness with Amnon she experienced shame, guilt, betrayal, resistance, exploitation, revulsion, rejection, loss, and intense grief.

The problem with these associations is that they are usually carried forward into other relationships. We do not have the end of Tamar's story. We are told only, "So Tamar remained desolate in her brother Absalom's house" (2 Samuel 13:20). Most abused people have significant problems in later relationships. The extent of these problems depends a great deal on how honestly the abuse and its consequences are faced. Tamar may have done better than some, because she was not hiding her feelings or dodging the ongoing effects in her life.

Negative feelings about closeness perpetuate the pain of abuse. Here is how it works: Many abused people are so humiliated and so shamed by the abuse that they try to forget it. They hate their memories. They fear exposure. They try to stuff their confused feelings into a back "closet" of their mind and lock the door.

This works for a while. Some people are able

to keep the closet door tightly shut for years. But life has a way of jerking doors open. A future relationship may not be abusive, but it will have tests. In some "insignificant" event, the closet door is yanked open, and out tumble feelings from the past. A surprised spouse, friend, or child becomes the object of intense negative feelings and hurtful actions.

That results in guilt. The abused person feels terrible for falling apart over such a small incident. He (or she) does not understand why he acted as he did. He hates himself for being so touchy, unpredictable, or explosive. This simply verifies that negative feelings have been associated with closeness and that healing has been delayed by denial.

5. *Tamar's abuse was painful because someone close to her minimized her pain.* As we have seen, Absalom responded by hushing Tamar and telling her it was nothing to worry about. "Hath Amnon thy brother been with thee? but hold now thy peace, my sister: he is thy brother; regard not this thing" (2 Samuel 13:20). Absalom knew better. He was so angry he wanted to kill his brother, but he stuffed his own feelings inward and essentially asked Tamar to do the same. "Absalom spake unto his brother Amnon neither good nor bad: for Absalom hated Amnon, because he had forced his sister Tamar" (2 Samuel 13:22).

When abused people hear others minimizing the problem, their pain increases. They can't understand this response of well-meaning friends and relatives. They may think, *They don't really care. They don't want to know. Nobody understands.* This adds to the confusion, pain, and loneliness.

6. *Tamar's abuse was painful because of how it changed her.* Amnon, as typical abusers, no doubt viewed this as an incident that happened at a point in time. It was past and done. For Tamar, however, it was a turning point in life. In the few minutes it took Amnon to vent his lust, she was changed from a virgin to a violated woman. The private walls of her heart were broken down. From this point on she would never be able to offer herself pure and untouched to a man. She felt like damaged goods. She faced any future relationship with the fear of rejection.

Tamar's abuse was a one-time incident. She was apparently physically mature at the time. There are many who have been abused as children; some repeatedly; some not by brothers but by fathers; some accompanied with much physical pain; some accompanied with threats, promises, or a confusion of love and hate; some with other kinds of trauma. As the details of abuse vary, so the pain varies, not only in kind, but also in intensity.

9

When sexual abuse occurs in children, for example, the confusion is greater. Tamar knew what Amnon was doing, but even so it was a painful confusion of love and selfishness. For a child who does not understand what is happening, this confusion is multiplied. Tamar's story does not tell us all the pain that can be associated with sexual abuse, but it shows the pain typical to an abused person.

How does sexual abuse affect people in ongoing ways?

The main events of Tamar's story are told, but much is discreetly left unsaid. Even less is said about what followed in Tamar's life. We wonder what all may have been included in that one word depicting the rest of her life: DESOLATE (see 2 Samuel 13:20).

The following points describe the emotional and relational desolation many sexually abused people experience:

1. *An inability to distinguish between real and imagined guilt.* An abused person normally feels tremendous shame. The difference between shame (having been involved in something shameful) and guilt (having done something sinful)

becomes blurred. Often such a person feels it was at least partly his fault. For example, Tamar might have thought, *If I had just not been so kind to Amnon. If I had not been wearing my best clothes. I probably said or did something that made Amnon want me.* Such reasoning is common for the sexually abused, but it is almost always distorted and often totally untrue. The abused person usually needs help in learning how to distinguish true guilt from imagined guilt.

2. *An emotional deadness.* As we have noticed, an abused person does not always respond wisely to painful inner feelings. An abused person may try to shut off all painful feelings—to feel nothing. One part of the mind wants to replay the incident because the hurt is a constant reminder of what happened. Another part of the mind screams NO! For some people, the emotional deadness is general, dulling virtually all poignant feelings. For others, it may be only toward certain people or in certain situations. Repressing one's painful feelings over a long period of time eventually shuts down other feelings as well.

3. *An inability to build emotionally close and satisfying relationships.* An abused person often sets up protective barriers to avoid getting hurt again. Ironically, the barriers that keep others out serve to shut the abused person in. The result is loneliness. The abused person often endures

for years the misery of feeling shut off from real and deep relationships. Meaningful interaction with other people is too risky.

4. *Distrust, especially with sharing deep feelings.* This is closely tied to the former problem. Meaningful relationships depend on trust. An abused person finds it easier to distrust than to trust, easier to hide than to open up, easier to suppress than to express, easier to put on a front than to be real. It is hard for an abused person to believe that another person will not take advantage of that which is private or personal. To share deep feelings is difficult and threatening.

5. *Panic in certain circumstances, often related to closeness.* An abused person consciously or subconsciously fears he'll be abused again. When the abuse was forced, as in Tamar's case, powerlessness is often a predominant feeling—there was just no way out. The abused person easily feels panic when he feels trapped. Some abused persons can't enjoy a hug, even in a good relationship where a hug is legitimate. Others do not experience panic in closeness with a marriage partner, but do when it looks as though there is no way out. They may struggle with making a decision, for example, because once the decision is made, they feel locked in.

6. *A feeling of distance toward God; an inability to feel close.* This can happen consciously or subcon-

sciously. Many people abused in close relationships find it hard to trust God, especially if their abuse took place in a supposedly Christian setting. If God would allow a brother such as Amnon to abuse his innocent sister Tamar, can she trust Him? Underneath many an abused person's anger toward the abuser is anger toward God. Until that anger is honestly faced, we cannot learn to know God, much less love Him.

In other cases, barriers toward God are subconscious extensions of barriers toward people. As an abused person shuts himself off from people, the protective habits may extend to God also, without the abused person being aware of it. An abused person wants assurances before he will trust. He guards against being vulnerable. To trust an invisible, nontangible Being feels too threatening. Inner warning lights flash when such a person tries to get close to God. For an abused person, the primary obstacle to drawing near to God may not be a matter of surrendering the will, but of crossing emotional hurdles.

7. *An inability to receive love (although it is craved).* This emotional paradox has a variety of causes. First, there is often the feeling of worthlessness that accompanies abuse. The abused person feels expendable and used—"How could anyone really love me?" Second, there

13

are the protective barriers. The abused person looks at love with suspicion. Kindness may be a trick. Warmth may mask hidden motives. Thus, suspicion often kills love before it can prove itself genuine. Finally, there is the abused person's anger. All abused people need to deal with anger. In Tamar's case, we see it most clearly in Absalom, but Tamar felt it at some point also, and no doubt in a more personal way. Some people handle their anger better than others, but anger destroys love. The abused sometimes find themselves in that confusing and frustrating situation of lashing out at those they need most. They easily develop love/hate relationships. They can't understand themselves. They have a deep hunger for love, but push away anyone trying to show love.

8. *A strong tendency to perform for acceptance; hold unattainable personal standards; are intolerant of personal mistakes.* A focus on performance grows out of feeling rejected. The abused person feels this is one way to gain approval. Because rejection has been so painful, acceptance becomes priceless; and an abused person will go to great lengths to get it. When performance is viewed as the means to acceptance, perfection is the only acceptable measure of performance. Unfortu-nately, perfectionists eventually apply their standards to others. This leads to the next point.

9. *A sudden spill-out of anger toward children.* This is usually in spite of determining "things will be different in my home." The spill-out of anger on children may have several causes. First, there is the "closet" problem, explained earlier. The anger has been shut up for years. The child is receiving what was originally felt toward the abuser, only grown worse with time. Then, there is the frustration of the abused person trying to keep his world safe through flawless performance. Little imperfections become major irritations. The child receives anger because his misbehavior feels threatening to the perfectionist parent.

10. *Friendships guided more by fear than by love; insecurities with others.* As we have seen, abused people find it easy to suspect others' motives. They easily allow fear to control them in other ways: 1) They may fear being abandoned; so they "check up" on their friends. 2) If a friend shows sympathy and understanding, the abused person may fear healing because the friend may then be unneeded. 3) The abused person may fear being "too much" for the friend to handle emotionally, and subconsciously he tests the friend by calling at inconvenient times, for example. If the friend shows any sign of being inconvenienced, the abused person is hurt and suspects the friend doesn't really care.

15

11. *A tendency to control, to try to make his world "safe."* Abuse knocks the bottom out of personal security. Only God can restore that security at its deepest level. But an abused person typically tries to make life safe. He tries to avoid closeness with anyone who might disappoint or hurt him. In seeking friendship, he leaves as little to chance as possible, even to the point of obligating his friends to fulfill the normal responses and interchange of friendship. Ironically, this actually increases insecurity in the friendship. When we obligate a friend, we take the voluntary factor out of the friendship—which in turn can leave us wondering if the person is really choosing to be friendly. Control tactics are never productive. On the surface, they get us what we want, but underneath, they destroy what we want most.

12. *An inability to have fun, to relax and enjoy any activity.* Some abused people find it difficult to let themselves enjoy life. This often goes along with a deep sense of guilt or shame or worthlessness. "I'm not worth anything" translates into "I'm not worthy of anything." This kind of person doesn't like to receive gifts, turns aside compliments, and feels some kind of inner atonement in hardship or trial.

13. *Great difficulty in making decisions; never done weighing all the possibilities; but often getting trapped in difficult relationships or situations, sometimes simply*

by default. As we noted earlier, decisions are difficult for a person who fears being trapped. But when decisions are avoided, they may be made by default. The course forced upon us when we avoid choosing a course gives the same trapped feeling. A person who avoids making decisions regularly looks back and wishes he had. But once in that pattern, he finds it hard to break. The feeling of being trapped through default only seems to confirm the danger of making a wrong decision.

14. *An inability to have healthy thoughts or feelings about sex; sometimes having periods of intense curiosity or preoccupation with sex; other times intense revulsion.* A sexually abused person often finds the thought of sex revolting. At the same time, he or she may have emerging sexual desires. (Depending on the situation, sexual desires may be normal, damaged, or perverted.) For a sexually abused adolescent, however, attraction toward the opposite sex triggers memories of abuse and usually results in confusion. Probably nowhere is the ambivalence of push/pull or attraction/revulsion felt more than in the area of sex. Some people are able to rise above it through the security of a loving, understanding partner. Others struggle for years. Some handle the ambivalence through masturbation. They relieve the "pull" of their sexual drives in the safety of aloneness, in a fantasy world where

17

they don't get hurt; but the thought of intercourse with a real person is terrifying or repulsive. In actual relationships they "push" others away.

Abused persons do not experience all these results, and what they do experience is not always in the same intensity. But all abused people need to work through some kind of ongoing consequences. Most people need the help of others to do so. The greater the problem the greater the need for wise, loving help.

In the next section we will examine steps that can help those who have been sexually abused.

PART 2
Steps to Healing and Hope

In Part 1, we looked at what abuse is, why it is so devastating, and how it affects people in ongoing ways. The account of Tamar comes from a historical section of the Bible, not from a teaching section, so we are not told there what to do for help and healing. The Bible does present God's remedies for the needs of mankind, however, and it offers help that is real and practical.

To get the most out of this section, you should have a notebook and be prepared to work through the suggested exercises under the heading "For you to do." Most people also profit from discussing with someone the material and the personal questions it raises.

What hope is there for the sexually abused?

"I am the LORD that healeth thee" (Exodus 15:26).

Let's begin this section by standing back, as it

were, and looking at God's power at work in the lives
of His people. What comes to your mind first when
you think about men such as Job, Abraham, Joseph,
Moses, David, Daniel, and the Three Hebrews? What
stories do you think of when you hear the name
Rahab, Ruth, Hannah, Esther, Mary Magdalene,
Lydia, or Dorcas? With just a brief mental review of
these people's lives, we can make some profound
observations about God:

1. God's power is demonstrated best in human
   need.

2. God often reveals His power and wisdom
   through situations that look impossible.

3. When God's people feel devastated, ruined,
   and worthless, God is able to bring out of
   their lives a message of His grace, wisdom,
   and power.

The Apostle Paul came to the place where he
actually rejoiced in his own weaknesses and needs
because he knew they provided opportunities for
Christ to reveal His power. "Most gladly therefore
will I rather glory in my infirmities, that the power of
Christ may rest upon me. Therefore I take pleasure
in infirmities, in reproaches, in necessities, in perse-
cutions, in distresses for Christ's sake: for when I am
weak, then am I strong" (2 Corinthians 12:9, 10).

The sexually abused have not necessarily suffered
for Christ, but they have suffered. And the same faith
that releases the healing, saving power of God for
the persecuted is necessary to release His healing,

saving power in the lives of the abused.

Jesus is the believer's Hope in all situations. He is the Healer. He can turn wounds into reminders of His grace. He can deliver prisoners from "unbreakable" bonds. He can show a clear path through chaos and reveal a wise plan beyond our "disasters." He said to Paul, "My grace is sufficient for thee: for my strength is made perfect in weakness" (2 Corinthians 12:9).

As we consider steps to healing and hope for those who have been sexually abused, let's keep our hope in this Lord. He is our Healer.

Healing is a process. We are "fearfully and wonderfully made" (Psalm 139:14), and nowhere is this more evident than in the healing process. As with physical healing, emotional healing usually takes time. And as with healing in the body, there can be complications, setbacks, improper diagnoses, quack remedies, and treatments that cause more harm than good; so it is with emotional healing.

With a broken bone, we need someone who is able to set the break. We may need a cast or a splint. With a bad break, we may need an operation using pins, plates, or screws. Certainly then, we need time for healing before we can use the limb properly. Even after the bone is healed, we may need therapy to restore muscle tone. In all this process, God is the healer. The doctor doesn't heal, nor does the operation or the cast or the steel pin. Each step is taken in cooperating with the healing process. But God is the healer.

21

Sometimes God intervenes and gives instantaneous physical healing. Even so, He sometimes gives immediate healing to those who have suffered sexual abuse. But more often, He works through a healing process. And He uses people to aid in the healing.

The healing process for sexual abuse can be divided into four steps. Some of these are more important than others, depending on the situation. Some steps take longer for some people than for others, depending on the severity of the abuse or what "complications" may have set in.

Step One: Honestly face what happened.

In Part 1 we studied the story of Tamar. As clearly as we can tell, Tamar faced her pain squarely. She tore her clothes, put ashes on her head, and wept. There was no hiding her abuse in a back closet of her heart. In years to come, her story became part of Jewish history.

Most sexually abused people would not want their story told for anyone to read. But for healing to take place, telling *someone* is an important part of the process. It is a way to face honestly what happened.

One way to do this is to *write down* what happened. This can be very painful for the abused person. Some people struggle through anguish and tears to write out the painful truth. Others prefer to talk it out. Some have trouble remembering more than vague details. Others were abused over such a long time in so many ways that memories run together. Hiding the abuse away in the heart only prolongs healing and complicates the problem. The longer it has been hidden, the harder it is to face it honestly.

There are extremes on either side of facing painful experiences honestly. On the one side is denial of the pain (locking it into one's closet). On the other side is looking at it constantly and using it to one's advantage. To such a person, the abuse is not locked away in a closet, but carefully kept in a "treasure chest." Either in secret or in the company of "trusted friends" (or both), this person reviews the array of hurts accumulated in the treasure chest. This is not facing honestly what happened, for the motives are not honest, pure motives. Review for review's sake, for selfish ends, for blame's sake, for self-pity, or for manipulating others, is unhealthy. It is not a step toward healing.

Sometimes a sexually abused person does not know if he has taken Step #1 properly. He wonders, *Have I looked at it enough? Have I looked at it too much?* One way to tell is to begin the next step. Each of these four steps builds on the former steps. Inability to take the next step (inability, not unwillingness) may indicate there was a problem with an earlier step.

For you to do.

The following questions may be helpful in facing what happened, whether you write it out or tell it to a friend:

1. How old was I when the abuse happened?

2. Where did the abuse take place?

3. Who was the abuser? (If there was more than one on separate occasions, take them individually and face what happened with each one.)

4. What did the abuser do?

5. Were other persons involved, and how were they involved?

6. How often did this occur, or over what period of time?

7. What did I say or do in response to the abuser?

8. What did I do in response to the abuse? (Note on these last two questions: This is not asking how you felt so much as what you said or did, although there may be some overlap. How you felt will be explored in Step #2.)

Step Two: Honestly face yourself.

There are four major questions to explore in facing yourself:

Question #1: *How did the abuse make me feel?*

In Tamar we see an emotional honesty. She did not deny her pain. She did not turn to escape tactics. Tamar wept. We see this emotional honesty often in the Psalms. Sorrow, grief, penitence, distress, loneliness, frustration, and confusion are expressed frankly in the Psalms. This emotional honesty is in the context of prayer to God as well as expressions of trust in the Lord and praise to His name.

The sexually abused person is certainly included in the exhortation, "Trust in him at all times; ye people, pour out your heart before him: God is a refuge for us" (Psalm 62:8). Pouring out our heart can be painful—more painful even than looking honestly at what happened. Sexual abuse is a loss. It is like a death. Tamar was not overreacting in her sorrow. She was being honest.

Again, writing is one way to face honestly how sexual abuse makes a person feel. If writing comes hard, find someone who can listen with understanding and who can ask appropriate questions.

Facing our feelings honestly saves us from the emotional and spiritual danger of repressing these feelings inside. David describes the effect of trying to "stuff" his powerful guilt feelings. "When I kept silence, my bones waxed old through my roaring all the day long" (Psalm 32:3).

Note carefully, however, that in the Bible, this emotional honesty is linked to a trusting relationship with God and godly people. Outside of that context, emotional expression can easily be nothing more than venting one's feelings. And although this may "connect us with ourselves" and avoid the consequences of repressing our feelings, it does nothing to connect us to God, the Healer and Restorer of our souls.

God does use His people to help the hurting and confused. Expressing our deep feelings to godly friends is Biblical. David had Jonathan, for example. And when Job was in distress, he longed for friends who would hear his distress and understand him. Job also shows how devastating it is when a person is emotionally honest and his friends misjudge him instead of listening compassionately.

Expressing feelings is easier for some people than for others, depending on one's personality, the nature of the abuse, and how the abused person has responded. A shy person may find it difficult to confide in others or may just find it difficult to express his feelings. If a parent was the abuser, the abused person may struggle with a sense of betrayal if he talks about his feelings. It feels like he is blaming the parent or talking about him behind his back. If the abused person has suppressed his feelings for years, he may be at a loss to know how he really felt.

Facing one's feelings may come by stages, particularly if the feelings have been blocked out for a long time. Feelings "frozen" inside may "fall off in chunks" as the door of the heart is kept open. The important thing is to keep the door open. Some people have lived behind a protective front. They may smile or chuckle in describing the abuse, when actually they have deep distress. This simply verifies the need to face one's feelings honestly in a safe setting. The chuckle is unreal. Tears of sorrow or anger have been squelched. Such a person can usually describe a huge or painful "knot" inside. Keep the door open. In a setting of love and honesty, the knot eventually unravels. When emotional honesty is regained, the relief is incredible.

For you to do.

1. One way to face how you feel is to sit down with a trusted friend and discuss point by point the section "How does abuse affect people in ongoing ways?" (from Part 1).

2. The following exercise may be another way to face your feelings. Each of the following emotions and feelings is often associated with sexual abuse. Circle the words best describing the intensity with which you felt them.

Shamed: mild, moderate, severe, never, seldom, at times, often

Dirty: mild, moderate, severe, never, seldom, at times, often

Used: mild, moderate, severe, never, seldom, at times, often

Worthless: mild, moderate, severe, never, seldom, at times, often

Powerless: mild, moderate, severe, never, seldom, at times, often

Angry at the abuser: mild, moderate, severe, never, seldom, at times, often

Angry at God: mild, moderate, severe, never, seldom, at times, often

Resentful: mild, moderate, severe, never, seldom, at times, often

Hateful: mild, moderate, severe, never, seldom, at times, often

Self-hatred: mild, moderate, severe, never, seldom, at times, often

Humiliated: mild, moderate, severe, never, seldom, at times, often

Betrayed: mild, moderate, severe, never, seldom, at times, often

Excited: mild, moderate, severe, never, seldom, at times, often

Afraid: mild, moderate, severe, never, seldom, at times, often

Confused: mild, moderate, severe, never, seldom, at times, often

3. As you look over the preceding list, what have been the most significant changes in your feelings in the time since your abuse?

4. For each of the feelings you marked as being "severe" or "often," what comes to your mind when you recall the feeling? Write it down or talk about it with someone.

Question #2: *How did I handle my feelings?*

The feelings associated with sexual abuse are vivid and painful. Often the abused person doesn't know what to do with these intense feelings. The hurt and confusion are real, but shame forbids the heart to open up and seek help. Following are typical methods people use to cope with these feelings:

1. *Denial.* This is the "closet" approach. Out of this come many everyday ways of avoiding painful issues. A person in denial may withdraw into a shell when threatened. He may avoid "feeling" as much as possible and just try to "get on with life." He may look blank, act dumb, wear a fake smile, or show no expression at all. He will likely refuse to trust, refuse to talk about deep feelings, and refuse to get close in relationships. He may act tough or uncaring or unhurt even when he is in extremely stressful situations. He's not showing his true feelings. He lives behind a front.

2. *Escape*. The person who escapes finds another "world" that feels safer or more pleasurable to avoid the real world's pain. This may be accomplished through fantasizing, reading, watching movies, taking drugs, listening to music, eating, masturbating, or by going after various pursuits with all his energy (business, recreation, health fads, sports, hobbies, religion, schooling, etc.).

3. *Blame*. This response rises out of the "treasure chest." The hurts become choice morsels to chew on mentally to ease the pain. The wrongs of others are always somewhere in view, no matter what the activity or discussion. The blamer is not always talking about the other's wrongs directly—many times it is only reflected in how a situation is described or not described, what is emphasized or de-emphasized. But this person finds his pain soothed to see faults and wrongs in others. This is very subconscious. The person who blames will often declare (and believe) he has not talked to anyone about the wrongs of others, but by hint or by insinuation, directly or indirectly, he has.

4. *Control*. The abused person typically has a fear of being vulnerable. Without realizing how he is doing it, he resorts to control tactics. Control tactics include not only taking charge of situations or people directly, but also

making others feel guilty, fishing for compliments, making others feel obligated, being possessive in friendship, playing the martyr, "sharing" excessively, and giving gifts in a way to obligate.

5. *Compensation.* Everyone who has been sexually abused struggles with shame. They often cannot distinguish between shame and guilt. To cope with these powerful emotions, they may try to compensate. Some become perfectionists in their standards for themselves and/or for others. Others compensate by trying to accomplish more than their share, by doing it faster or better, or by being able to handle any problem or challenge. Some turn to prayer, Bible reading, or sacrificial service. They often do not realize what is driving them, but it is the desire to rid themselves of the awful feeling of shame.

For you to do.

Sit down with pencil and paper or with a trusted friend and discuss each of the preceding methods of coping. Start by looking at which method is *most* characteristic of you and which is *least* characteristic. Then go on to discuss each one.

The following questions may further help identify and evaluate the way you cope with your feelings:

1. When did I first feel shame?

2. When did I feel used?

3. How have these feelings grown or diminished since the abuse?

4. What kind of masks have I worn?

5. How have I wanted people to view me?

6. In what kinds of situations could I find relief from my feelings?

7. Did I live in an imaginary world? If so, what was it like?

8. Did I try to confide in anyone? How did it go?

9. How much, when, and where did I cry?

10. Do I try to appear more "tough" than I really am?

11. Am I ashamed of tears? Afraid of tears?

12. What fears have I had?

13. To what extent have I gone "round and round" in my mind reviewing what the abuser has done to me?

14. To what extent have I mulled over the implications of my abuse (how it has "ruined" me, how it has affected what others think of me, etc.)?

15. Do I often feel left out, an oddball?

16. How do I feel when I make a mistake others see?

17. In what ways do I perform for the approval of others?

Question #3: What unhealthy responses have I developed?

Feelings are powerful motivaters. The intense feelings associated with abuse are not only difficult to live with, but they easily become the basis for our behavior. For this reason, abuse is a hotbed for carnal, unproductive responses. Even when we think we have shut off and stuffed our feelings down to nothingness, they are affecting our behavior. In fact, the feelings pushed out of our awareness are the most dangerous, because not only are they "out of sight," but their effects on us are more subconscious.

Facing myself this way is difficult and painful. The tendency is to kick and fight against coming to the light. Abuse makes us feel rotten anyway, and to have to acknowledge that we have developed faults that added rot in the process, feels humiliating.

But such honesty is also rewarding. By looking at our wrong, unproductive responses, by taking personal responsibility for our behavior, and by applying God's grace, we can begin repairing the damage. There are blessings in being real. There is hope when we can recognize barriers, blame patterns, and manipulation. The bones that were broken can rejoice when we see wrong patterns replaced with righteous responses based on the Word of God and motivated by the love of God.

For you to do.

Identifying your unproductive responses will take time. As you walk with God, He will continue to show you yourself and your need of change. An abused person usually needs a committed helper to be a sounding board for identifying wrong responses. Without guidance, you will tend to be too hard on yourself in some areas and totally miss areas of real need.

The following questions can serve as a guide for looking at yourself. As you read through these questions, mark the ones that stand out to you as being problems. Next, have your helper mark any he thinks you missed. Then begin working your way through by then either talking about or writing out your response to each question.

1. In what way do I avoid personal responsibility?

2. What kind of defenses do I use when I feel the threat of blame?

3. How do I respond when people get too close to me?

4. To what extent can I be honest with others about my personal needs?

5. Do I avoid making decisions? If so, how has this affected others?

6. How do I typically respond under pressure?

7. In what ways do I make others uncomfortable when they get close to me?

8. Can I listen sympathetically to people's problems without needing to tell them my problems? (That is, sharing my problems with a hurting person only if it will benefit that person.)

9. Do I talk so much or so little that I make others uncomfortable?

10. Have I damaged my views about sexuality by reading sinful literature or by fantasizing?

11. When I am hurt, how do I affect those around me? Do I get silent, loud, critical, or intolerant?

12. Am I demanding of others?

13. Do I make allowances for others the way I want them to make allowances for me?

14. Am I easily offended?

15. Do I allow others to do things for me? Am I a gracious receiver? If not, what hinders me?

16. Do I make much of my troubles? Do I find secret satisfaction when others notice I am in trouble, and do I harbor secret resentment

when they do not notice? (Note: It is right to appreciate when fellow Christians care, but it is not right to demand that they care, nor to use our trouble to measure whether they care.)

17. Have I made critical generalizations about the opposite sex?

18. Have I made vows in times of resentment or disappointment about how I will or will not relate to other people?

19. Do I make others feel guilty when they disappoint me?

20. Do I make others feel obligated to help me?

21. Am I possessive in friendships? Can I allow them to be close to others without feeling personally threatened?

22. Do I flatter my friends?

23. Do I "rank" people in importance by their looks, education, wealth, or manners? And to what extent do I allow this to affect my kindness and respect for them as persons?

24. In what ways do I hold people at a distance who should be close to me?

25. Do I talk to numerous people about my problems?

26. Am I intolerant of mistakes in others? How do I let them know how I feel?

27. Do others catch the spill-out of my inner turmoil and anger?

28. Do I make belittling comments about myself or things I do?

29. How do I respond to compliments?

30. How do I respond to criticism?

31. Does everything have to be "just right" when I am working with others?

32. Do I try to win or keep my friends by making sacrifices for them or by doing things for them? How do I feel when they notice? When they don't notice?

33. On what does my personal sense of security/insecurity hinge?

As you identify problem areas, you can develop a work-list for personal growth. For example, you may find that you need to work on 1) being less demanding, 2) learning to receive graciously, 3) being more sensitive to the feelings of others, 4) being receptive to criticism, and 5) not being such a perfectionist that others are uncomfortable working with you. If you feel discouraged, keep in mind that everyone struggles with these kinds of things, but abuse intensifies the struggle.

Don't fear the light. Welcome it. If you get bogged down here, you may want to study John 3:19-21 or 1 John 1. Or it may be helpful to take breaks from self-analysis by focusing on the Lord, what He has done for you, and what He means to you.

It takes wisdom to see oneself. And it takes time to allow God's Spirit to sanctify the heart, renew the mind, and change the behavior. All your unproductive response patterns don't need to be changed before you go on, but you need to start by honestly facing them. The next step, "Facing God," will continue the process.

Question #4: To what extent did I participate?

For some abused persons, this question is entirely irrelevant, even offensive. Theirs was a Tamar experience. They were completely unwilling participants. But even unwilling participants struggle with guilt feelings. Some agonize over questions such as, "Did I somehow invite the abuse?" Or they may repeatedly lament, "If only I would have been wearing something different," or, "If I had not smiled, it probably wouldn't have happened." Tamar could well have had similar thoughts following her abuse. For those forced into sexual contacts, facing this question honestly can relieve much false guilt.

Abuse has many variables. Some situations begin with innocence for both parties and only later move into the awareness that something is wrong. Some abused persons raise a protest. Some protest too late. Some do not protest, but do not like what is happening. Some have conflicting feelings, such as a certain pleasure mixed with guilt. Some participate willingly for a time. Some fully enjoy what is happening, and even initiate it at times.

How does a person sort through all this? This can be a very confusing issue, but it is part of honestly facing oneself.

For you to do.

To work through this issue wisely, answer the following questions, noting the explanations accompanying them. You might also discuss the questions with someone.

1. *How old was I at the time?* Incidents during the innocence of childhood must be viewed differently from incidents that happen after we know what we are doing.

2. *Who was the "leader" in the encounter?* Sometimes children explore and discover themselves and one another in mutual innocence. The encounter is abuse when an older one takes the initiative and a younger one follows. Sometimes, however, a younger person is more sexually informed or more physically mature and takes the lead. For anyone leading the innocent into sin, Jesus said, ". . . it were better for him that a millstone were hanged about his neck, and that he were drowned in the depth of the sea" (Matthew 18:6). Clearly, the leader bears responsibility.

3. *Who was used in the encounter?* This is similar to the above question, but it further helps to determine responsibility. In most abuse, an

older male uses a younger female, but sometimes it is reversed. When an innocent boy is introduced to sexual activity by an older sexually wise girl, he is being abused, even if he enjoys it. His innocence is being exploited for someone else's selfish pleasure.

4. *When did I become aware it was wrong?* Sometimes what began in innocence continues after one is aware. Although another may be responsible for abusing me and shares responsibility for dragging me into the involvement, I am responsible for wrongdoing I willingly took part in after I became aware it was wrong.

5. *Did I ever initiate an encounter?* Initiating wrong behavior in innocence is different from initiating wrong behavior in awareness. What I initiated in awareness, I am responsible for.

6. *Who had the ability to stop the encounter?* If two are approximately equal and there is an awareness of wrong, the right response is to say no as Tamar did (see also Deuteronomy 22:23-27). Tamar could not stop Amnon, however, even with being his approximate equal. Children being used by an older person are far less able to stop what is happening. Even when a child's verbal protest might stop the older one, the child may choose not to protest because of his innate tendency to submit to an older person, particularly if that person is a family member. A child should never be made to feel guilty for

41

not stopping the initiatives of an older abuser.

7. *Did I hide my involvement in order to continue it?* This question may reveal a great deal about the level of participation. A child may not tell his parents about the abuse (even though he hates it) for a variety of reasons:

a. The abuser commits him to secrecy through threats or bribes.

b. The abuser is someone the child wants to protect.

c. The child feels guilt and fears punishment.

d. The relationship with the parents is distant or strained.

e. There is a hidden understanding (or misunderstanding) that "you just don't talk about such things in this house."

f. The child simply does not know how to handle the confusion.

All of these reasons are different from the motivation of a willing participant who enjoys what is happening and wants to hide it from authorities. If that is the case, the person needs to take responsibility for his participation and not hide behind the willingness or the initiative of the other person (again see Deuteronomy 22:23-27).

Where there has been willing participation in

immoral behavior, even though it began with unwilling participation or abuse, we must take responsibility for the behavior. This will be covered more clearly in Step #3.

8. *Did I act or appear in provocative ways?* Let's set several things straight before looking at the question. First, the Bible says, "Unto them that are defiled and unbelieving is nothing pure" (Titus 1:15). A lustful person can be aroused by virtually anyone. That Tamar was the object of Amnon's sexual desire, in other words, does not in itself mean she did anything to cause that. Second, being attractive does not constitute provocation. Tamar was beautiful, but as far as we know she was innocent. Third, even provocative behavior does not justify sexual abuse. What Amnon did would have been reprehensible even if Tamar had flaunted her beauty. Fourth, the point of facing this question is not so much to establish blame as it is to identify and correct immature or unhealthy ways of relating.

But now to speak to the question: Sometimes young women do talk, walk, laugh, or dress in ways that invite the attention of men. Girls who grow up with poor relationships with their fathers may be especially "hungry" for the attention of boys. They may knowingly or unknowingly handle their bodies to that end—not consciously asking for sexual intimacy, but calling for attention, and being misread by lustful men. Again, misconduct never justifies abuse. But facing our appearance, our conduct, and how we relate to the opposite sex is part of a mature, honest look at ourselves. To weigh this question wisely often takes the perspective of someone who can look on objectively and be both honest and loving.

Sorting through one's responses is time-consuming and very personal. This process, however difficult it is, will always prove worthwhile. By honestly facing oneself, much of the uncertainty and insecurity is laid bare. The unknown becomes clearer. The fear-filled eyes begin to focus on something manageable.

Step Three: Honestly Face God.

Many who have suffered sexual abuse struggle with anger toward God. The abuse has been so painful they cannot get away from the big question, "WHY did God allow it to happen?" When they do try to get close to God, they may face emotional barriers, erected either in anger or fear. Against all those emotional objections, the truth still stands: WE NEED GOD.

The Bible addresses fallen man's pitiful response to God in one short clause: "There is none that seeketh after God" (Romans 3:11). In spite of man's sin, need, emptiness, and multiplied problems, and in spite of God's cleansing, fullness, forgiveness, and ability to do more than man can ask or think, our tendency in times of trouble is to go our own way, find our own solutions, and run our own lives. Ironically, the very trouble that can turn us from God if we listen to our own hearts can turn us toward God if we listen to the call of God's Spirit.

The truth is we cannot solve our own problems. The truth is we are utterly dependent on God. The sooner we turn to the Lord and humbly acknowledge our need of Him, the sooner we can find help.

The abused person may be coming to God primarily to find answers. In his pain and confusion, he may not see past his longing for healing. But God wants us to find more than answers. God wants us to find Himself. One of the joys of turning to God for help is the profound realization that there is far more to God than healing. There is far more to Him than answers to our problems. There is far more than His supply for our needs. There is GOD. Glorious He is! All-powerful and worthy of the praise and worship of every creature He has made. When we see beyond our momentary need of Him and glimpse Him, we cry out with the hymn writer, "O for a thousand tongues to sing/My great Redeemer's praise!"

This great God uses our pain and our trouble, however, to bring us to Himself. The psalmist said about the Israelites, "Then they cried unto the LORD in their trouble" (Psalm 107:6). We begin this section by exploring five reasons why the abused person needs to turn to the Lord:

Reason #1: *We must turn to God for cleansing.*

"If we confess our sins, he is faithful and just to forgive us our sins, and to cleanse us from all unrighteousness" (1 John 1:9).

The abused do not need cleansing from the abuser's sin. For some, this is a difficult distinction, as we noted earlier. But there are times when the abused has been a participant in the sin to some degree. This can be acknowledged honestly to God. Furthermore, as we have seen, the abused person often responds unwisely to the pain. These unwise, unproductive, even sinful responses can likewise be brought to God. If we have been angry or resentful, if we have been reclusive and distant, if we have lashed out at people, if we have been angry at God, if we have refused love from those who really do care, if we have become controlling, if we have lived behind a front, if we have had wrong concepts about our sexuality, GOD KNOWS all about these things. The best we can do is to bring these problems to Him honestly and humbly. He has been waiting for that to happen, and He does cleanse us from ALL sin.

For you to do.

On a separate sheet of paper, make a list of the wrong ways you responded to your abuse. Be specific. Be thorough. But be accurate. If you are prone to being hard on yourself, check this list with a trusted friend before proceeding. Then bring this to the Lord, read it to Him, and ask Him for His forgiveness and cleansing. Tell the Lord you are open to His ongoing work in your life, and thank Him for hearing your prayer.

47

Reason #2. We must turn to Christ for our security.

"Christ Jesus . . . is made unto us wisdom, and righteousness, and sanctification, and redemption" (1 Corinthians 1:30). Because of Jesus Christ, I have become a new creature (1 Corinthians 5:17). I died with Him, was buried with Him, was raised with Him, and am now seated with Him in the heavenly realm (Ephesians 2:1-6; Romans 6:1-4). In Christ, I have no condemnation (Romans 8:1). In Him, I receive all spiritual blessings, I am chosen, I am predestinated for eternity with God, I am redeemed and forgiven, and I am sealed (stamped) as God's own through the indwelling Holy Spirit (Ephesians 1:3-14).

Sexually abused persons typically struggle with insecurity. They may resort to control tactics in an effort to make their world safe. Or they may look for a sense of security in something tangible, such as their friends or their performance.

Jesus said, "Come unto me, all ye that labour and are heavy laden, and I will give you rest" (Matthew 11:28). We receive rest for our souls by a living, spiritual union with Jesus. He is our safety. He is our security. In Him we can rest.

For you to do.

Learning to know Christ as our security takes time. To explore this profound and glorious reality, look up each of the Scriptures that follow and write down what Jesus is to you personally:

1. John 1:29 Jesus is _____ .
   He is the One sufficient, complete sacrifice for my sin, reconciling me to God through His blood.

2. John 6:35 Jesus is _____ .
   He is able to satisfy my inner hunger completely and give me the nourishment I need for spiritual growth.

3. John 10:7 Jesus is _____ .
   Through Him, I EXIT the heartache and sorrow of self-centered living, and I ENTER the security and protection and provision of His fold.

4. John 10:11 Jesus is _____ .
   His leading is always right and His protection is always safe.

5. John 14:6 Jesus is _____ .
   He is my Guide and Example in every situation; He is everything I believe in; and He is all that I ever want to be.

6. John 15:1 Jesus is _____ .
   Everything sweet and good that comes from my life has its origin in Him.

7. Matthew 9:15 Jesus is _____ .
I am betrothed to Him for eternity.

8. Romans 8:29 Jesus is _____ .
In my heavenly family, He is my oldest brother, the One we look up to and honor.

9. Ephesians 2:20 Jesus is _____ .
My life is built firmly on Him, so that in storm or earthquake I rest securely on Him.

10. 1 Timothy 2:5 Jesus is _____ .
Because of Him, I need never fear the wrath of God for my sin.

11. Hebrews 4:14-16 Jesus is _____ .
He has experienced earthly trials and knows exactly how I feel. He can faithfully represent me and my needs to my heavenly Father.

12. Hebrews 12:2 Jesus is _____ .
He is at the beginning and end of all that I believe, and He will bring my faith to maturity.

13. 1 John 2:1 Jesus is _____ .
In heaven my righteous Saviour stands in my behalf when I sin, fail, or make a mess of things.

14. 1 John 2:2 Jesus is _____ .
His sacrifice is abundantly sufficient for the gigantic "stack" of this whole world's sin. I can thereby be assured that He is able to forgive mine.

15. 1 John 5:12 (see also Colossians 3:4) Jesus is

_____ . All my spiritual vitality, strength, wisdom, and righteousness come from Him. Because He lives in me, I am spiritually alive; without Him, I am nothing and can do nothing.

16. Revelation 1:8 Jesus is _____. He is the center of God's purposes from start to finish.

17. Revelation 19:16 Jesus is _____ . He is over everything and everyone—highest, greatest, mightiest, most glorious—now and forever.

To further cultivate your sense of security in Christ, you might try taking one of these truths each day. Thank God for what Jesus means to you. Write out what it means to you personally to know Jesus in this way.

Reason #3: We must turn to God in order to change.

"But we all, with open face beholding as in a glass the glory of the Lord, are changed into the same image from glory to glory, even as by the Spirit of the Lord" (2 Corinthians 3:18).

For the sexually abused, change can be both longed for and dreaded. The inner misery and problems resulting from the abuse cry out for change. But to move out from behind the protective habits, the "shell" of loneliness and the "safe" barriers can be scary.

We need God for such changes, for several reasons. First, it is only in His light that we can properly see what needs changing. Second, we need God because He is the only one with whom we can ever be absolutely safe. Humans fail. They grow weary. Their love stretches thin. Their wisdom is limited. God does work through His people, and the sexually abused need mature people of God, but in the center of their heart they need God for their security, their safety, their Rock to stand upon. And third, only God has the power to actually change the heart of man. Humans can give good advice. They are able to "plant and water the seed." But only God can give "the increase" (1 Corinthians 3:6).

For you to do.

Following are typical changes needing to happen in the life of an abused person. Mark the ones that describe your need for change:

_____ a. I need to be less suspicious, and more trusting of others.

_____ b. I need to rest in the Lord instead of desperately taking situations into my own hands.

_____ c. In my relationship with God, I need to

move away from placing security in my performance, and I need to trust in Christ.

_____ d. I need to learn how to take barriers down instead of putting them up.

_____ e. I need to cultivate right attitudes about myself.

_____ f. I need more structure and personal discipline in my life.

_____ g. I need to be more patient with others, less demanding, and less easily irritated.

_____ h. I need to be more emotionally honest.

_____ i. I need to be real with people instead of hiding who I am.

_____ j. I need to receive love graciously and trustingly.

_____ k. I need to think of others' needs, not dwell on my own.

_____ l. I need to take down the front of _____
_____ .

_____ m. I need to replace unhealthy attitudes about sex with healthy attitudes.

The following questions may help you to further evaluate your need for change and to bring your needs to the Lord:

1. As you look at the needs you identified above,

53

which seems most threatening to you? Why does it feel threatening?

2. Which seems most difficult?

3. How do you honestly feel about changing in these areas?

4. How will change in these areas affect your relationship with God?

5. How will changes affect your relationships with others?

6. What needs to happen in order for you to change?

7. To what extent do you have control over or responsibility for these changes? Are you willing to do what you can to bring about change?

On a separate sheet of paper, write out a prayer to God expressing the need for changes in your life, telling God of your willingness to change and giving Him the freedom to lead you in making these changes however He sees best.

*Reason #4: **We must turn to God as the object of our faith.***

"But without faith it is impossible to please him: for he that cometh to God must believe that he is, and that he is a rewarder of them that diligently seek him" (Hebrews 11:6).

Spiritual progress begins and ends with God. Only by faith can we reach Him. Only by faith can we walk with Him. Only by faith can we know His power and grace and love in our hearts.

The sexually abused need eyes of faith. They need to see first that God IS. They need to see that God is sovereign. They need to see that in His sovereignty God does allow evil in this world. He has chosen to allow people to act wrongly, speak wrongly, decide wrongly, and plan wrongly. God allows abuse to happen. The evil in this world is not outside of God's sovereignty—He does not cause evil, but He allows it to happen.

We do not know all of God's reasons for allowing evil. But we do know that God's grace and God's power and God's wisdom are big enough to bring deliverance out of this world's evil. "Where sin abounded, grace did much more abound" (Romans 5:20). Those who have been abused need eyes of faith that can begin to perceive this marvelous grace of God. Out of their wounds, God is able to bring healing. Out of their tragedy, God is able to bring hope. Out of their chaos and confusion, God is able to bring order. Out of their shame and misery, God is able to bring a testimony of His glorious grace, power, and wisdom, "that we should be to the praise of his glory" (Ephesians 1:12).

For you to do.

To cultivate your faith, complete the following activities:

1. Read Isaiah 61:1-3. From verses 1 and 2, list the kinds of people Jesus is able to help.

    a. _____

    b. _____

    c. _____

    d. _____

    e. _____

2. From verse 3, list the transformations God is able to bring about for these people.

    a. _____

    b. _____

    c. _____

    d. _____

3. According to this verse, what results when God works in the lives of hurting people?

    _____

    _____

4. Begin a list of good things God has brought about in your life or things you trust He will bring about in your life as a result of your abuse.

Reason #5: We must turn to God in order to forgive the offender.

"Our Father which art in heaven . . . forgive us our debts, as we forgive our debtors. . . . For if ye forgive men their trespasses, your heavenly Father will also forgive you: But if ye forgive not men their trespasses, neither will your Father forgive your trespasses" (Matthew 6:9-15).

This is a very difficult step for many who have been sexually abused. The abuse is so wrong, and the abuser may seem so selfish and wicked that forgiving him can seem not only unreasonable, but impossible. That is exactly why we must turn to God. Without Him, forgiveness depends on human effort, is limited by human reasoning, and ends in human failure.

Note here that forgiving the offender is under Step #3, "Honestly face God," rather than under Step #4, which will be "Honestly face the abuser." Forgiveness is something we must do in response to God before it is something we can do in response to man. We must settle it on our knees with our face toward God.

Because forgiveness is such an important part of healing, and because it can be so difficult in actual experience, let's look at it more closely.

Understanding forgiveness:

Let's begin with the words of Jesus: "Then said he unto his disciples, It is impossible but that offences will come: but woe unto him, through whom they come! It were better for him that a millstone were hanged about his neck, and he cast into the sea, than that he should offend one of these little ones. Take heed to yourselves: If thy brother trespass against thee, rebuke him; and if he repent, forgive him. And if he trespass against thee seven times in a day, and seven times in a day turn again to thee, saying, I repent; thou shalt forgive him. And the apostles said unto the Lord, Increase our faith" (Luke 17:1-5). From this teaching, we can make a number of observations:

> a. *Forgiveness is for wrongs.* This point may seem self-evident, but many people stumble over it. They find it hard to forgive an offense for which there was no justifiable reason, and was "so wrong." But that is exactly the point of forgiveness because sin is wrong forgiveness is necessary.
>
> Forgiveness does not mean, "I approve." It is not saying to the offender, "It's okay. What you did is all right." Forgiveness does not minimize wrongdoing. Rather, forgiveness allows us to look squarely at sin and know it is wrong.
>
> b. *Forgiveness does not take away the need for rebuke.* Notice that Jesus actually linked forgiveness with rebuke. Forgiving the offender does not

take away the need to deal with his sin in the church. It does not take away the need to set up restrictions in his activities or relationships. It does not take away the reality of his crime or that there will be consequences for it, perhaps even legal charges.

c. *Forgiveness means release on a personal level.* By the act of forgiveness, the one offended is turning the offender free "between you and me." On that personal level, he is saying, "I am not going to hold this on my account against you. I am releasing you." It is like the release of obligation to pay a debt (see Matthew 18:21-35). The offended one will no longer personally "charge" the offender.

d. *Forgiveness stops the snowballing effect of anger and hurt.* The alternatives to forgiveness are anger, blame, revenge, grudges, ill will, gossip, hatred, and multiplied hurts. If we respond to injury with injury, we only add to the problem. Forgiveness does not always stop the injury—we may need to forgive "seven times in a day"—but by forgiveness we are at least not contributing to the problem.

Understanding how to forgive:

a. *Forgiveness is possible by faith in God.* After Jesus talked to His disciples about forgiveness, they said, "Lord, increase our faith." The tie between forgiveness and faith must not be overlooked. Faith is the primary means of forgiveness. We are able to forgive ONLY as we change our focus from the offender to God. We develop a positive attitude about what God is able to do in our lives (even through the abuse), in place of a negative attitude about what the offender has done. Through our faith in God, we are able to release the abuser. Included in this is the awareness that *God considers offenses serious business.* Jesus said it would be better to drown under the weight of a millstone than to face God as an offender of "little ones." We can rest assured that God will take care of all unrepentant abusers. This leaves the abused free to forgive.

b. *Forgiveness is possible as we view our own need of forgiveness.* All people stand in need of God's forgiveness. And although some sins have more interpersonal consequences in this life, all sinners stand under the eternal death penalty. All have sinned, and all need the Saviour. Jesus pointed out numerous times that our own need of forgiveness should teach us to forgive. When we see how much we need it, how can we withhold it from others?

c. *Forgiveness is possible as we consider the worth of our forgiveness.* Because we needed to be forgiven, Jesus died for us. His death in our behalf has spared us from hell. Not only so, it has promised us heaven, eternity with God. If we suffered abuse all of our seventy years on earth, terrible as those years would be, they would not compare to what we are spared from through Christ, nor to what we have been promised. In light of Calvary, in light of a burning hell, in light of a glorious heaven, we can forgive.

d. *Forgiveness is possible only if I choose to forgive.* It takes more than my choice to forgive—it takes the grace of God and the power of God and the wisdom of God. But I cannot forgive unless I choose to do so. I must be willing to forgive. This is what Jesus meant when He said, "from your hearts forgive" (Matthew 18:35).

For you to do.

Some people find it helpful to start the forgiveness process by writing down the names of the people involved in the abuse (each one on a separate sheet of paper). Under each name, list the things that person did, and then take this in prayer to God. Read what is on the paper and tell the Lord, "By Your grace, I am choosing to forgive _____. I will no longer hold this on his account. I choose to believe You are able to heal me and use me for Your glory." When each person has been forgiven, physically destroy the papers. This can be done in the presence of witnesses, or it can be entered in one's journal as a witness that forgiveness has begun.

Learning to believe in God, experiencing life through faith in Him, forgiving the abuser through faith in God—these are processes. They take time. They come about as we have the courage and persistence to face God honestly. To conclude this section, let's look at several pointers that can help in facing God:

1. *Be absolutely honest with God.* Tell Him who you are, what has happened to you, and how you have responded.

2. *Keep a journal.* For many people it helps to write down their thoughts and feelings through the time of healing and change. Write out your "letters" to God, your prayers, your feelings, and your commitments. If writing comes hard, try talking to a friend and have your friend keep notes, so you can later refer to helpful insights.

3. *Keep your heart cleansed.* Do not allow evil thoughts, resentment, unbelief, or despair to reside in your heart. As you begin the healing/changing process, honest confession of failure and need may be a daily work. Never despair. God knows, and He understands the intents of your heart.

4. *Continue the study of your spiritual union with Christ and your security in Him.* The Scriptures given earlier on this point can be a starter for you. Look them up. Write them down. Study them. Meditate on them. Memorize them. Paraphrase

them. Claim them. Make them part of your daily thoughts, and build them into your heart.

5. *Exercise your faith.* Faith grows as we read God's Word (Romans 10:17). Faith grows as we express it (Romans 10:9, 10). Faith grows as we fellowship with other believers (Acts 2:42). Again, it is helpful to keep a written record of your faith. Tell God what you learn about Him from Bible stories. Express to Him your faith in Him. You may do this even when your heart is flooded with misery or failure. Following is an example:

> Lord, I am discouraged. A man innocently leaned close to me today to help me with my work, and I panicked. I hate men all over again, and feel so vulnerable and afraid. I sometimes wish I were not a woman. But I know that no matter how I feel, You understand me. You made me. You made me a woman, and though I don't understand all of Your purposes, I choose to believe that You are good. I believe You have purposes for my life. I am trying to find those purposes, and I believe that even out of the abuse in my life, You are able to bring a message of Your grace. Please cleanse me of my anger and deliver me from my fears.
>
> I know there are many hurting people. I know they need to learn to know You

as their Healer and as their God. If you can use my life to show them that message, I give you freedom to do that in any way You choose. You are right and good. You are completely trustworthy, and I am devoted to You. Your daughter,

_____.

6. *To further build your faith, begin a collection of verses that help you trust in the Lord.* For example, Isaiah 26:3, 4; or 41:10. Many of the psalms describe the faithfulness of God and His ability to help His people in times of trouble. For example: Psalms 34, 37, 42, 103, and 139.

7. *As you experience growth with God, keep a list of insights you receive.* Begin a list of good things God can bring out of your abusive past. Add to these lists as the Lord teaches you, and be willing to share these blessings with others at appropriate times.

Step Four: Honestly face the abuser.

Facing the abuser is the last of the four steps. This step takes us in a new direction and often raises questions. How necessary is it to face the abuser? Can the abused person find healing without taking this step? What are the Biblical reasons for taking such a step? If a person has healed quietly without facing the abuser, is it necessary to "dig it all up again"? What if the abuser is dead? What if the abuser's whereabouts are unknown? Or what if the abuser is not a Christian?

This guide was written primarily to help those who have been abused, and especially for adults abused in their childhood. This guide takes into account that most abuse is committed by a family member or someone close to the family. For those recently abused, or for adolescents, or for those whose abuser is a stranger or is facing criminal charges, there are factors to consider beyond those presented here.

Let's begin in the Word of God. In both Testaments, we find that one's sexuality is precious and needs to be protected. A sexual relationship between a man and a woman forms a bond and an awareness between them that makes their relationship unlike any other relationship. The Bible refers to it as "knowing" one another. The bond of intimacy may be attractive and positive when love is present; or it may be repulsive and negative, as in Tamar's case where lust took over. It was because of Amnon's twisted and short-lived bond of intimacy with Tamar that she "remained desolate in her brother Absalom's house" (2 Samuel 13:20).

In the New Testament, Paul refers to the bond of intimacy when he warns, "What? know ye not that he which is joined to an harlot is one body" (1 Corinthians 6:16). This is not a marriage bond, but it is a joining, a shared experience of knowing one another so that those two people can never look at one another in the same way again.

In the Old Testament, when an unmarried man had sexual relations with an unmarried woman, he was obligated to take her for his wife (unless her father objected); and he was forbidden to put her away (see Exodus 22:16, 17 and Deuteronomy 22:28, 29). This law demonstrates the truth already stated: sexual intimacy constitutes a union, (not a marriage union), and forms a "knowing" between two people that has ongoing implications.

A primary purpose of a meeting between an abused person and the abuser is to face this reality. Rightfully, the abuser should initiate such a meeting, and some may do so. But as we have seen, the abuser typically sees this as an event in the past. He is usually unaware how the abused person has struggled against the union that occurred, and how that struggle has kept alive, from the abused person's standpoint, an awful bond.

Further, forgiveness, returning good for evil, or not prosecuting an eye for an eye does not take away the need to rebuke or to work through issues of wrongdoing. Jesus said, "If thy brother trespass against thee, rebuke him; and if he repent, forgive him" (Luke 17:3). To Jesus' disciples, the term "thy brother" likely was understood generally as a fellow Jew; later it came to be more specifically a fellow believer in Jesus. As such, it is a term that may or may not apply to one's abuser. Details such as who the abuser is and his relationship to the abused person certainly bear upon how an approach is made. But the point here is that a forgiving spirit is not in opposition to facing wrongdoers or dealing with their wrongdoing. Indeed, forgiveness gives proper goals and methods for doing so.

Does everyone need to take Step Four to experience healing? Certainly not. Some will never be able to because the abuser is dead. For others, he or his whereabouts may be unknown. Where there is no ongoing interaction with the abuser, a meeting is less important. But when there is ongoing interaction, as there usually is, arranging a meeting with the abuser to clear up the relationship can be part of the healing process for the abused person.

To make this a profitable meeting, the abused person needs the preparation of the first three steps. There are dimensions to Step Three, "Facing God," that will never be complete in this life, so in one way, the abused person is never "ready" for facing the abuser. But until the abused person faces God and finds healing and cleansing taking place, he is certainly not ready. It takes discernment to know when the time is right. Reading through this section will help in making that decision.

1. The purposes for facing the abuser need to be clear.

First, we need to understand that the purpose of facing the abuser is not to accuse. It is not to dig up the past and throw it in his face. It is not to punish the abuser, get even with him, or shame him.* Many times the abuse has not been addressed since it occurred. Occasionally an apology took place if the abuse was found out, but normally the abuser has little idea what the abused person has gone through since the abuse. Sometimes the abuser and the abused person have frequent contact (for example, at family gatherings), and both may have a vague uneasiness—neither knows what the other remembers, nor do they know how the other one feels about it with the passage of time.

---

* (There is a valid place for confronting the abuser and dealing with his wrongdoing, especially if it happened recently or if the abuser has not changed his ways. Dealing with transgressors, however, is best handled by proper authorities, such as family heads, church leaders, or civil authorities, depending on the age of the abuser, his spiritual condition, and his relationship to the abused person. The Old Testament clearly teaches that justice is not the personal responsibility of the one wronged. And while the New Testament says civil authorities are given for protecting the righteous and punishing wrongdoers, it calls God's children to rise to ethics even higher than justice in responding to wrongs against them.)

Situations vary, and goals may vary also, but following are typical goals for a meeting between an abused person and the abuser:

    a. To honestly face a wrong that has had ongoing consequences.

    b. To give the abused person opportunity to describe the consequences that followed the abuse, and to give the abuser opportunity to face the suffering caused by the abuse. (Many abusers have little idea of the damage and pain they have caused.)

    c. To give the abused person opportunity to describe how he (or she) responded to the abuse and what he is doing to find healing.

    d. To give the abused person opportunity to express forgiveness to the abuser.

    e. To give the abuser opportunity to respond positively to the one he abused.

    f. To bring clarity to the relationship, so both are able to know it has been faced honestly and can be laid aside.

    g. Where necessary, to establish relationship boundaries to safeguard against further harm.

When Paul wrote to the Corinthians, he addressed the problem of a man involved in immorality and said the Corinthians were not dealing with this man adequately. Paul gave specific directions for this situation. In his second letter, after they had followed his instructions, he wrote: "For godly sorrow worketh repentance to salvation not to be repented of: but the sorrow of the world worketh death. For behold this selfsame thing, that ye sorrowed after a godly sort, what carefulness it wrought in you, yea, what clearing of yourselves, yea, what indignation, yea, what fear, yea, what vehement desire, yea, what zeal, yea, what revenge! In all things ye have approved yourselves to be clear in this matter" (2 Corinthians 7:10, 11).

This Scripture describes the clearing that took place when the church properly addressed a problem. While there would be differences between this situation and a meeting between an abused person and his abuser, the results can be similar, especially when the parties involved are in the church. Every effort will have been made to clear the past and make the present relationship healthy.

For you to do.

Before making any approach to your abuser, prayerfully consider the goals for doing so. Which of the above goals are most pertinent to your situation? Are there other dimensions in your life or your abuser's that call for additional goals? After you have considered these questions, write out your goals for such a meeting.

2. *The abused person should write out what he (or she) wants to say to the abuser.*

Writing it out allows the abused person to choose words carefully and accurately. It also leaves an accurate record of what actually was said in the meeting. A copy of the letter can be given to the abuser after the meeting, if he wants one. Following is an example of what might be said:

Dear _____,

I have a letter I want to read to you. Please let me finish before you ask any questions, and then if you want to make comments, you may.

I need to face with you an incident in our past and explain how it has affected my life, and what I am doing with it. It was many years ago, the evening you caught me alone, pulled up my dress and tried to have intercourse with me. I was so scared. Later that same evening, you tried again.

This may seem to you like an incident in the past and something that should not be brought up today. But for me, the effects have been ongoing, and I believe you should know.

I experienced a lot of conflicting feelings as a result of that evening—shame, fear, guilt, anger, and confusion. It was years until I really knew what you had done. I have felt dirty, but mostly I have felt used and worthless. And I have had bitter feelings toward you. I could not understand these feelings fully. I tried to shut

71

out how I felt. I tried to bury my feelings so I could go on with life.

But recently, by God's grace, I have been honestly facing myself and trying to deal with my emotional and spiritual needs. I have realized that God is using this pain and confusion in my life to draw me closer to Himself. He is healing me. He is helping me accept what happened. And I am praying He will continue to work in my heart and life.

I am not having this meeting to blacken your name or blame you, but to face honestly what happened and to help break the bondage that sexual abuse has held me in. I want to learn to trust God and others, to be able to be close to others in proper ways and have meaningful relationships. I want to be able to look you in the eye and know this has been dealt with. My prayer for you is that you, too, can face this and find freedom from any bondage this sin may have brought to you.

And so today I can say with an open heart, _____ , I forgive you. I will not hold this against you. And I ask you for forgiveness for the anger and unforgiveness I have had in my heart toward you.

As far as I am concerned, I am willing to lay this issue to rest between you and me.

Sincerely, _____

For you to do.

If you decided a meeting with the abuser should take place, write out a letter to use in such a meeting. You may use the above letter as a guide, but use your own wording. The content of the letter should include 1) a clarification of your purposes for the meeting—this may be all at the beginning or throughout the letter; 2) a summary of the abuse; 3) a description of how the abuse affected your life; 4) a statement telling what steps you have taken for healing; and 5) an expression of forgiveness to the abuser.

3. Arrangements should be made for a meeting with the abuser.

Besides the goals for this meeting and the letter, there are important steps that should not be overlooked. First, there should always be a third party involved. This person (or couple) should be a person whom both can respect (such as a minister or family head). He may be responsible for guiding the meeting.

Second, the meeting should take place in a neutral place, specifically not at the home of the abuser. The one who was abused may call for the meeting simply by saying to the abuser, "I have something I need to talk to you about. It is important to me. Could we meet at _____." In some cases it may be better for the third party to arrange the meeting (for example, if the third party is a minister, the abuser is a church member, and the matter concerns the church as well as the abused person).

Third, the abused person should read the letter to the abuser, give him a copy after the reading if he wants one, and wait for his response.

Fourth, the meeting should stick to the goals. If the abuser becomes defensive or accusing, the meeting should be brought to a close (or the third party may wish to talk further to the abuser). When the goals have been achieved, the meeting should end rather than drift aimlessly on.

Fifth, if restrictions are necessary in the relationship and if the abuser responds positively, the abuser should be informed of this need. After he has opportunity to think about it, another meeting should be arranged to work out these restrictions. If the abuser does not respond positively, the restrictions should be made according to the needs of the abused person, and the abuser should simply be informed.

For you to do.

To arrange for a meeting with the abuser, work through your third party—your friend, your pastor, or a family head. Go over the goals. Let this person read your letter and check for any unproductive attitudes, such as blame or self-pity. Then discuss the best procedures for arranging for the meeting.

Common questions about facing the abuser:

1. *What if the abuser is dead?* The abused person may write out a letter to God, following an outline similar to a letter to the abuser: 1) Stating what happened. 2) Acknowledging how he (she) responded to the abuse. 3) Listing what he is doing about it. 4) Expressing complete forgiveness to the abuser.

    Even though the abuser is dead, forgiveness needs to take place, and God is willing to hear such a statement of clearing. The letter can be read to God as a prayer in the presence of a third party. Although this does not verbalize anything to the abuser, it can provide an emotional "closure" to the abuse for the abused person.

2. *What if the abuser is not a Christian?* Most of the goals (listed under Point #1) are still important even if the abuser is not a Christian. The possibility of a wrong response may be greater, but the abuser should still be given the opportunity to respond.

3. *What if I have no further contact with the abuser, and don't even know where he lives?* The less frequently

there is contact, the less critical the need for facing the abuser. If there is little possibility of ongoing interaction, the abused person may write a letter to God (as above). Again, this can help to close off unfinished business.

4. *What if I don't think it will do any good?* The primary goals have to do with the abused person—taking a necessary "clearing" step in the healing process. The responses of the abuser are secondary goals. The abused person must be willing to accept the risk of being misunderstood. But he (or she) will have far more satisfaction in having faced the situation, having expressed what needs to be said, and having given the abuser the opportunity to face it, than in continued evasion and denial.

5. *What if the abuser said he is sorry after the abuse?* Genuine repentance must be acknowledged, but if the abuser apologized only at the time of the abuse and only for the incident and has never faced the ongoing effects for the abused individual, facing those effects is still in order.

6. *What if the abuser gets angry or refuses to admit wrongdoing?* One of the goals for meeting with the abuser is to bring closure to the violation of intimacy. Another is to clarify the relationship between the abuser and the abused. Both of these goals depend in part on the abuser's response. But even if the abuser responds wrongly, the personal goals of the abused

person can be realized. He (she) can still face the past, express forgiveness, and thus bring clarity to the relationship from his standpoint. A wrong response would be regrettable, but need not be devastating. Healing for the abused person does not depend on an apology from the abuser. Indeed, his (her) personal peace does not depend on anything external, including the worst imaginable response from the abuser. If there is an angry or accusing response, we have the clear teachings and example of Jesus. "Who, when he was reviled, reviled not again; when he suffered, he threatened not; but committed himself to him that judgeth righteously" (1 Peter 2:23). "Not rendering evil for evil, or railing for railing: but contrariwise blessing; knowing that ye are thereunto called, that ye should inherit a blessing" (1 Peter 3:9).

Summary

Abuse is a painful and confusing experience. How grateful we can be that God understands this and that He has made provision for healing, for cleansing, and for restoring relationships!

After seeing these Biblical steps to healing, some may look back on their experience and say, "Well, I was abused, and I didn't follow all those steps. Am I healed or not? Do I need to go back and go through this particular process?"

The most important issues to consider are not whether one has taken certain steps in a certain order. Even as some physical injuries heal without doing exactly "what the doctor ordered," so it is with emotional injuries. God is merciful and good. No doubt some people have found healing without ever writing anything down about their abuse or talking to another person about it. Conversely, others could work through the steps presented in this manual, as well as other material on sexual abuse, and prolong or hinder the process by focusing on it too much. There are issues more basic than whether one has followed Steps One through Four. The following questions may help to discern the more important issues:

1. Am I honest with myself, with God, and with others?

2. Am I able to feel the range of human

emotions without being driven by them?

3. Do I have a peace about my past, or does it still stir negative feelings in me?

4. Do I have an inner contentment, or is there unexplained unrest?

5. Do I have healthy friendships?

6. Can I easily relate to children?

7. Do I have abnormal panic around certain people or in certain situations?

8. Are my thoughts about my sexuality healthy, relaxed, and pure?

9. Do I have a growing delight in God?

10. Can I hear a sermon on any Biblical truth without inner reaction?

God wants His children to be honest. He wants them to have healthy and upbuilding relationships. Above all, He wants them to be learning to know Him. The goal of working through the damage of sexual abuse is not primarily for our personal happiness. Nor is it so we can feel better about ourselves or relate better to others. The primary goal of healing the wounds and taking down the unnecessary barriers is so that we can be restored to our God, so we can move into that limitless sea of knowing the One who made us and worship Him with a vibrant spirit, a restored soul, and a cleansed mind and body.

If this manual helps toward that end, it has accomplished its purpose. May the Lord's blessing and grace be with every person who has the courage to bring their wounds to the true Healer, and in the healing move on to the inexpressible delight of knowing God.

> Then they cried unto the LORD in their trouble, and he delivered them out of their distresses. And he led them forth by the right way, that they might go to a city of habitation. Oh that men would praise the LORD for his goodness, and for his wonderful works to the children of men! For he satisfieth the longing soul, and filleth the hungry soul with goodness.
>
> Psalm 107:6-9.

Christian Light Publications, Inc., is a nonprofit, conservative Mennonite publishing company providing Christ-centered, Biblical literature including books, Gospel tracts, Sunday school materials, summer Bible school materials, and a full curriculum for Christian day schools and homeschools.

For more information about the ministry of CLP or its publications, or for spiritual help, please contact us at:

Christian Light Publications, Inc.
P. O. Box 1212
Harrisonburg, VA 22803-1212

Telephone—540-434-0768
Fax—540-433-8896
E-mail—info@clp.org